How to Draw
BUTTERFLIES
and Other Insects

Peter Gray

PowerKiDS
press.

Published in 2014 by The Rosen Publishing Group, Inc.
29 East 21st Street, New York, NY 10010

Illustrations: © Peter Gray
Editors: Joe Harris and Nicola Barber
U.S. Editor: Joshua Shadowens
Design: sprout.uk.com
Cover design: sprout.uk.com

Library of Congress Cataloging-in-Publication Data

Gray, Peter, 1969–
 How to draw butterflies and other insects / by Peter Gray.
     pages cm. — (How to draw animals)
Includes index.
 ISBN 978-1-4777-1299-3 (library binding) — ISBN 978-1-4777-1409-6 (pbk.) — ISBN 978-1-4777
1410-2 (6-pack)
1. Insects in art. 2. Drawing—Technique. I. Title.
 NC783.G73 2014
 743.6'57—dc23

                                            2012047580

Printed in China
SL002499US

CPSIA Compliance Information: Batch #AS3102PK: For Further Information contact Rosen
Publishing, New York, New York at 1-800-237-9932

CONTENTS

THE BASICS

DRAWING

You should start your drawings with simple guidelines before fleshing them out with detail.

Build up the general shape of your subject with guidelines. I have drawn the guidelines quite heavily to make them easy to follow, but you should work faintly with a hard pencil.

Guidelines

Detail

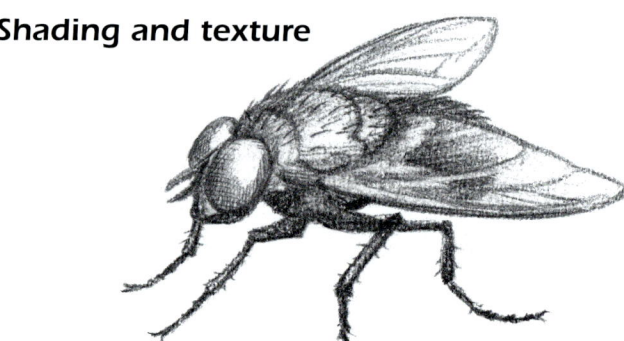

Use a softer pencil to develop the character and details. You may find that you do not follow the guidelines exactly in places. That's fine—they are only a rough guide.

Shading and texture

Carefully erase the guidelines and mistakes. Then add shading and texture with a soft pencil.

INKING

For a bold look, go over the outlines with ink. Wait for the ink to dry thoroughly, then erase all the pencil marks.

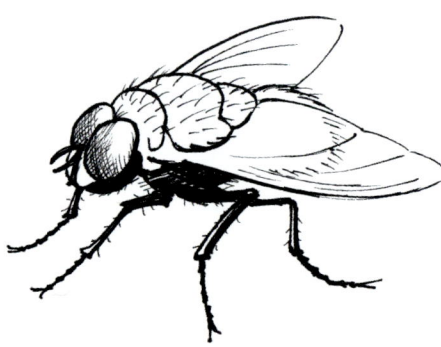

The easiest inking method is to use a felt-tip pen. If you plan to add paint at a later stage, make sure your pen is waterproof.

Felt-tip pen outlines

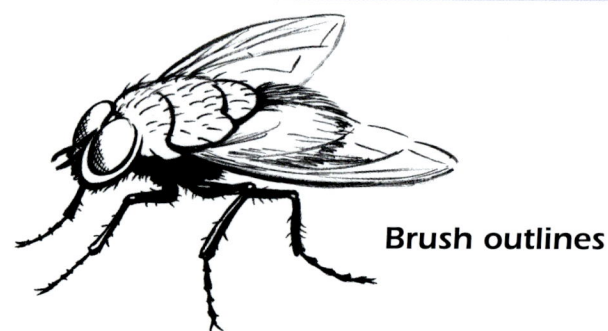

Brush outlines

For a more graceful effect, use a fine-tipped watercolor brush dipped in ink.

COLORING

Although I use watercolors in this book, the main principles are the same for any materials. Start with the shading, then add in markings and textures, and finally, work your main colors over the top.

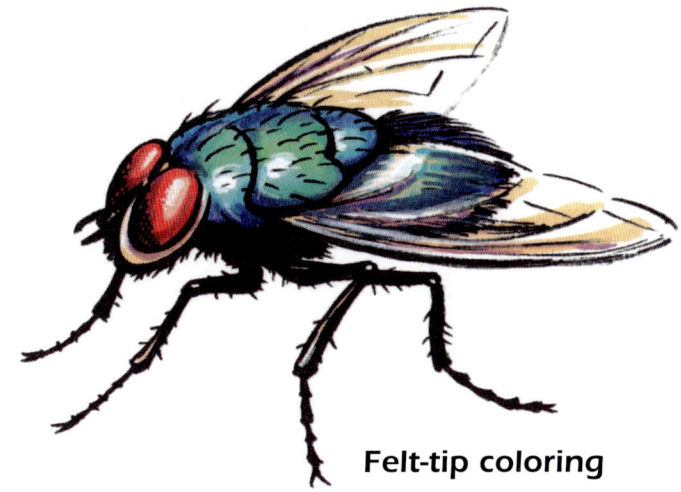

Felt-tip coloring

Felt-tip pens produce bright, vibrant colors. Work quickly so that the pen strokes do not remain visible.

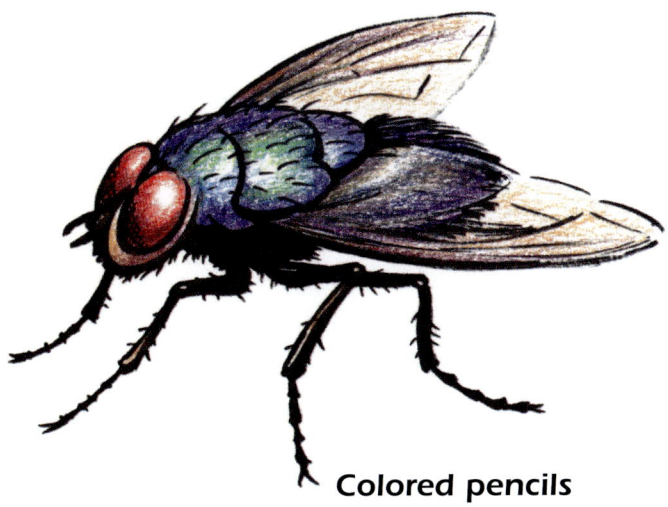

Colored pencils

Colored pencils are the easiest coloring tools to use, but you have to take great care to blend the colors to achieve a good finish.

Watercolors

The subtlest effects can be achieved with watercolor paints. It is best to buy watercolor paints as a set of solid blocks that you wet with a brush. Mix the colors in a palette or on an old white plate.

BODY PARTS

Before starting to draw insects, it is very useful to look closely at the construction of their bodies.

Insects have six legs. In many insects, the legs are joined to the body at the thorax, but beetles have legs joined to the abdomen. The legs are made up of several separate parts ending in very fine claws.

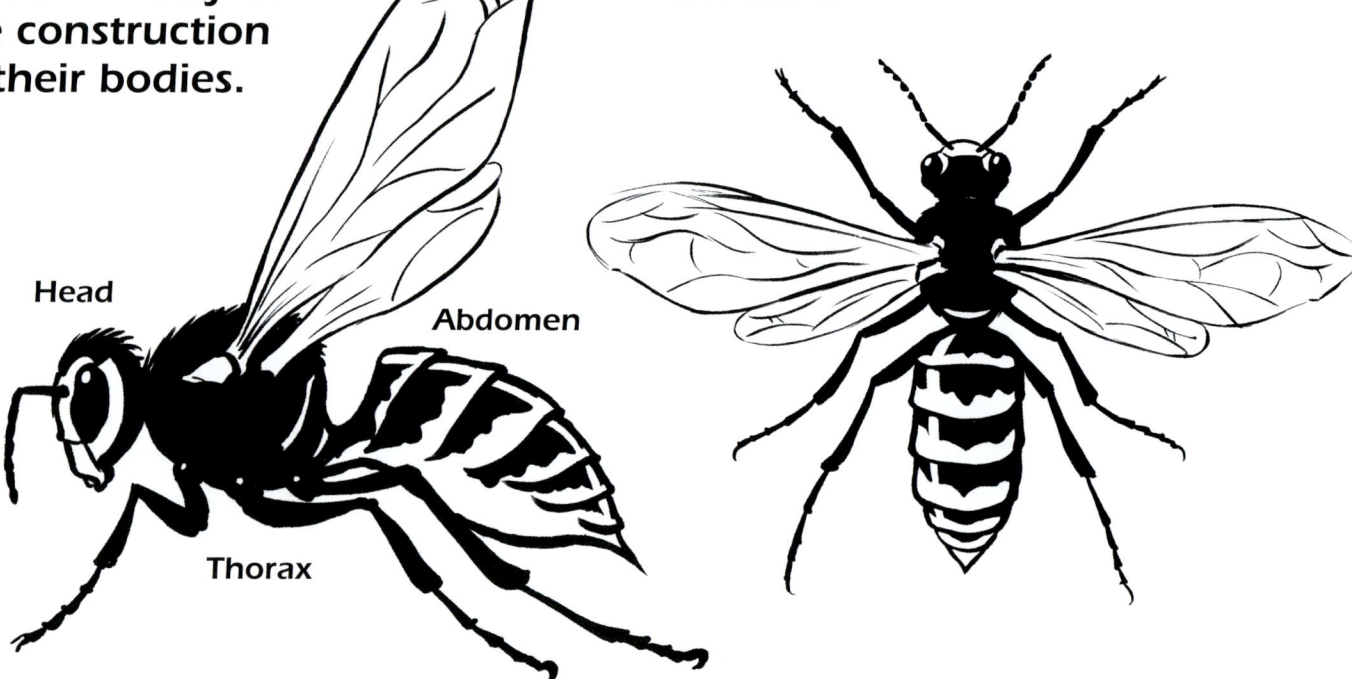

Head

Abdomen

Thorax

Insects' bodies have three sections: the head, the thorax (middle section), and the abdomen (rear part).

The wings are in pairs, with the front wings larger than the rear. They are also joined to the thorax.

WASP FACE

Insects usually have large eyes that sit apart on the front of the head.

The **antennae** come out of the forehead between the eyes. The mouthparts are jointed at the sides, so that the jaws move from side to side.

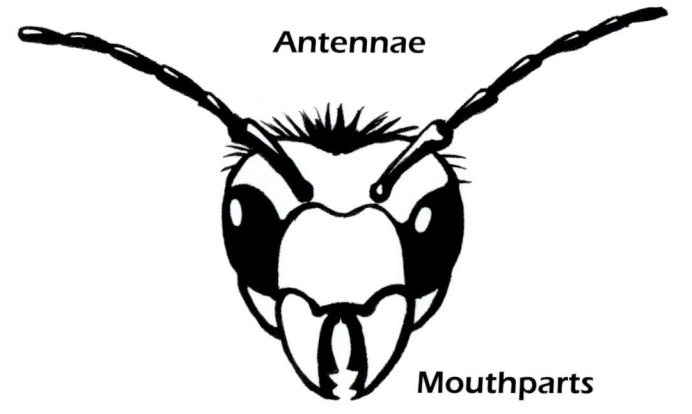

Antennae

Mouthparts

SHADE AND SHINE

To show an insect's shiny surface, you will need to use highlights. You will also need to apply shading to capture the effect of the insect's round body.

With neither shade nor highlights, this ladybug looks flat and dull, despite its bright coloring.

Apply shading underneath the main color. The shading need not be gray—you can use a **neutral** version of the main color.

The simplest way to make highlights is to leave parts of the drawing uninked and unpainted, but you need to plan this carefully.

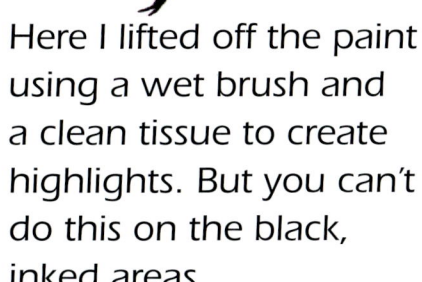

Here I lifted off the paint using a wet brush and a clean tissue to create highlights. But you can't do this on the black, inked areas.

Adding chalk or pastel highlights on top of a colored drawing can give good results, but it can be difficult to control the fine details.

The best method for adding highlights is using white ink and a fine-tipped brush. You can water down the ink for a more subtle sheen.

BUTTERFLY

There are many thousands of different types of butterfly, and they live in nearly all parts of the world. The striking shapes, colors, and patterns of their wings have inspired some beautiful butterfly names, such as "painted ladies," "hairstreaks," "coppers," "metalmarks," and "swallowtails."

1 Butterflies are **symmetrical** down a center line, so a grid is a helpful guide to start your picture. Use a ruler to draw two squares side by side. The center line is where the squares meet. Then draw more guidelines inside the boxes as shown. The lines do not have to be exact, so long as they are the same on each side.

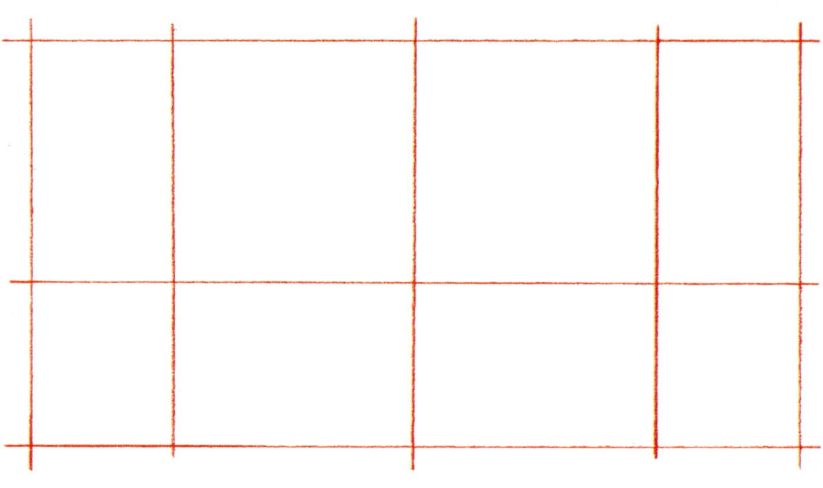

2 Working on either side of the center line, sketch in the three parts of the butterfly's body (head, thorax, and abdomen). Add the wing shapes with curves that fit inside the grid guidelines.

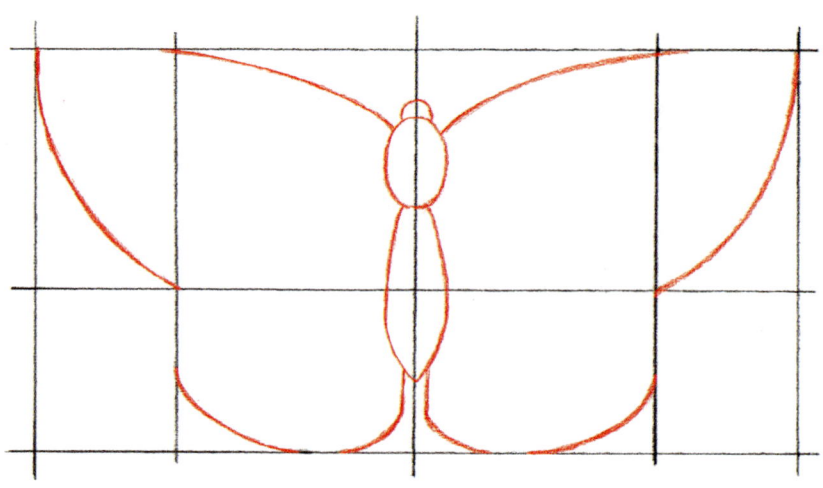

3 Draw the divisions between the wings, and then add the outlines of the wing markings, branching out smoothly from the thorax. I decided to draw the two antennae at slightly different angles, to break up the symmetry a little.

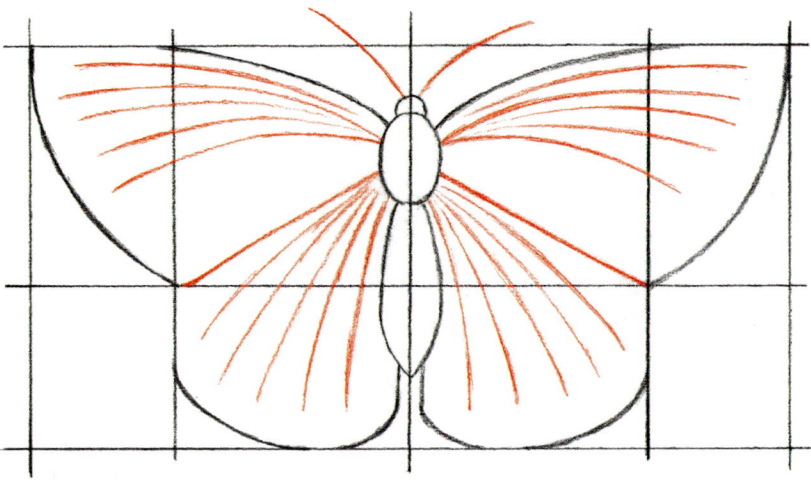

4 Work on the wing markings and the outer shapes of the wings. Then add some detail to the head and mark the curved divisions along the abdomen.

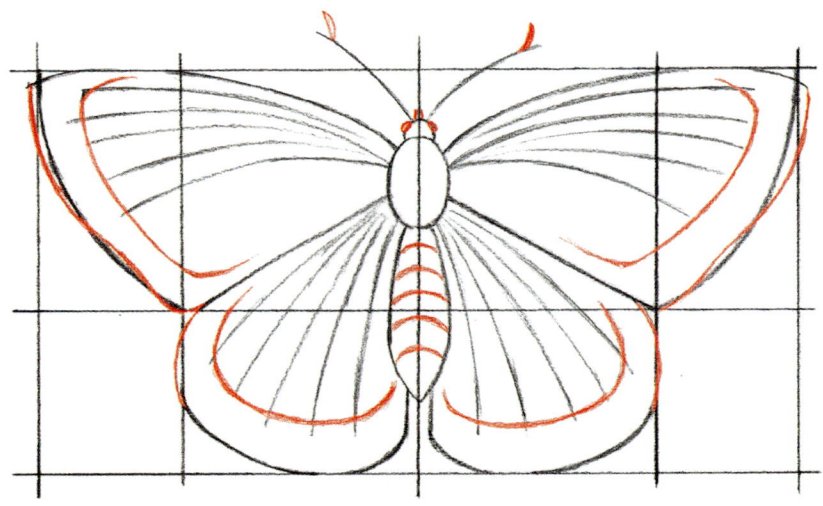

5 The grid lines will help you to place the finer details and markings of the wings symmetrically. Keep going from one side of your picture to the other, making sure each mark is followed by its mirror image.

6 For the inking stage, I used a rich blue instead of black, to avoid making the outlines too heavy. I inked in the darker lines of the body and the markings with the tip of a fine brush. Each time the brush started to run dry, I switched to more delicate markings. For the outer edges of the wings, I used tiny strokes of thin brown ink.

7 There is not much shading to be done on a relatively flat subject such as this. But a touch of purple or blue around the body and the inner parts of the wings gives the drawing some solidity and depth.

8 Now apply some color to the main parts of the wings to create a pattern. I used some pale pink with a fairly dry brush to stroke a subtle sheen on the inner parts of the wings. For the bolder outer markings, I avoided black paint, which would be too heavy here. Instead, I mixed up some brown and blue to make a dark shade.

TINY SCALES

Butterfly wings are covered in tiny scales so minute that the human eye can see them only through a microscope. They help to protect the wings. They also create the beautiful colors and patterns that we see on a butterfly's wings.

ANIMAL FACTS

9 For the main color, I mixed up a large batch of pale blue. The important thing here is to wash the color on quickly, so that you do not disturb the paint you have already put on the wings. Paint with a fairly broad brush, following the direction of the wing markings.

10 For the final detailed touches, I used some white ink and a very fine brush to lift out the delicate highlights of the wing markings. You can also add fine highlights to the fluffy thorax and the shiny abdomen.

STAG BEETLE

Stag beetles get their name from their large mandibles—the jaws that stick out from either side of the head—which look a little bit like the antlers of a male deer (stag). Only male stag beetles have these big mandibles. They use them for fighting other males over territory and mates.

1 Overlap the guidelines for the three body parts as shown. The abdomen and thorax are simple ovals, and the head is a semicircle. Be careful with the angles at which they join.

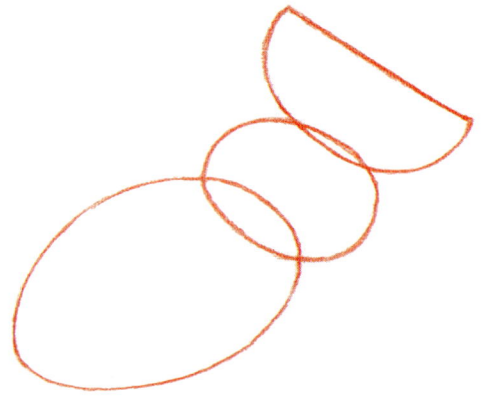

2 Draw a large oval shape to form the outline of the mandibles. To help position the legs correctly on both sides, draw them through the body. Add center lines curving over the thorax and the abdomen.

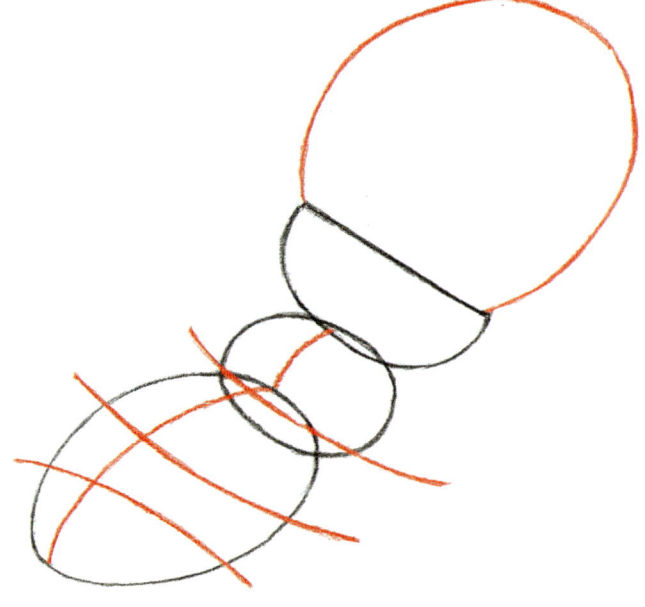

3 Extend the leg shapes with two further sections on each leg. Start to fill in the mandibles inside the large oval guidelines.

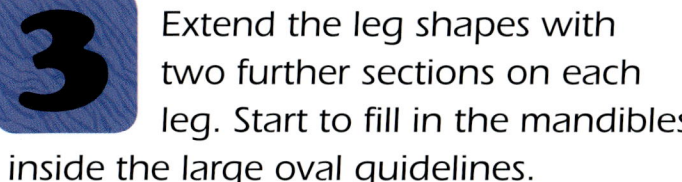

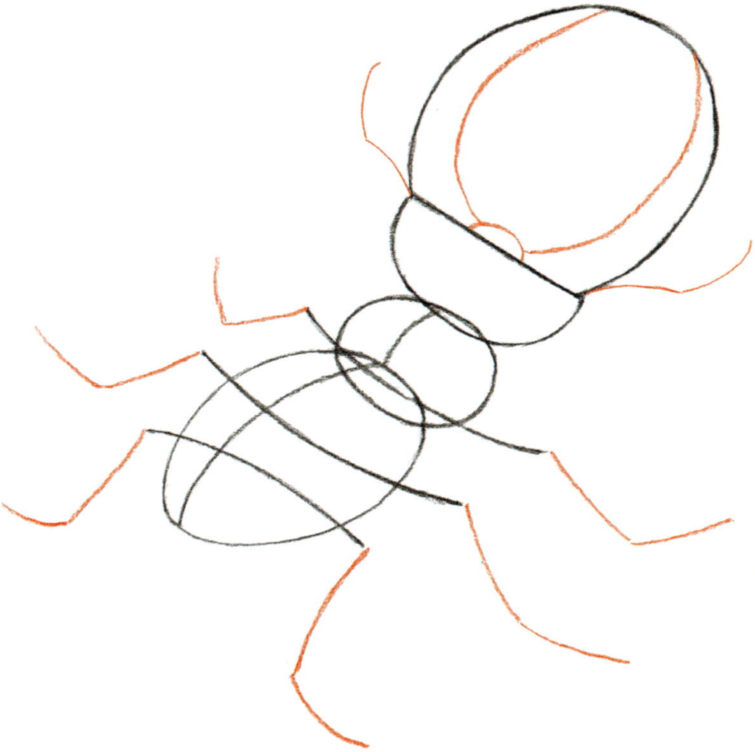

4 Add more detail to the shapes of the body parts and the mandibles. Give the legs some thickness and shape, and finish each foot with claws.

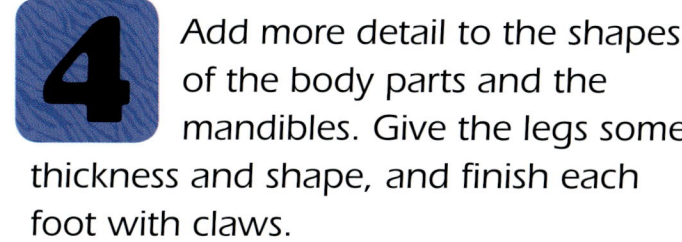

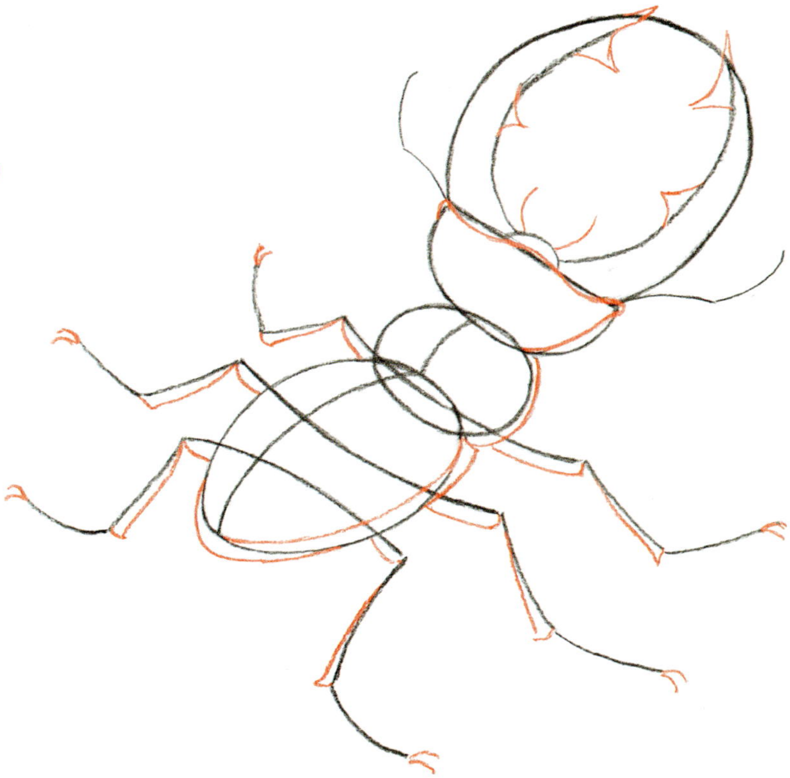

SLOW STARTER

Stag beetles start life as eggs, which hatch into tiny grublike **larvae**. The larvae live in rotten wood, which they eat to grow to full size. This can take up to six years! But when the fully grown adult stag beetles eventually come out into the open, their life span is only about six weeks.

ANIMAL FACTS

5 To develop your drawing, add fine texture and small details to the legs, mandibles, and antennae. This will help at the next (inking) stage.

6 I used black ink to outline this sturdy creature, making sleek unbroken lines with a fine brush. The lines can be heavier on the dark underside of the body. I colored in the full thickness of the legs with the black ink.

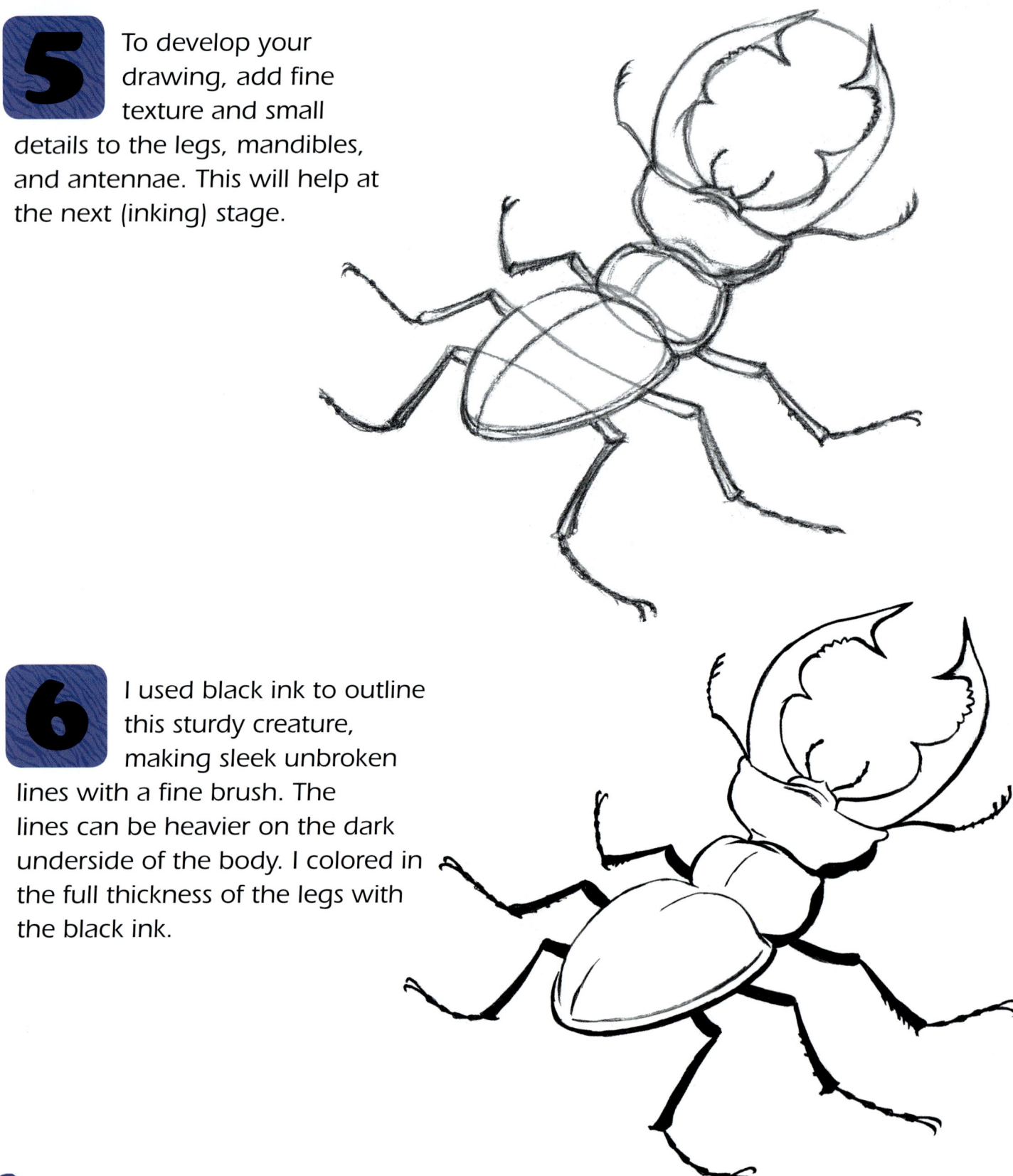

7 For the rich, dark color of the beetle's body and mandibles, I painted several layers of dark gray, purple, and deep red. Some delicate spots of white ink brought shine to the legs. For the highlights on the abdomen, I thinned the white ink down with water, then applied it in several layers for a textured sheen.

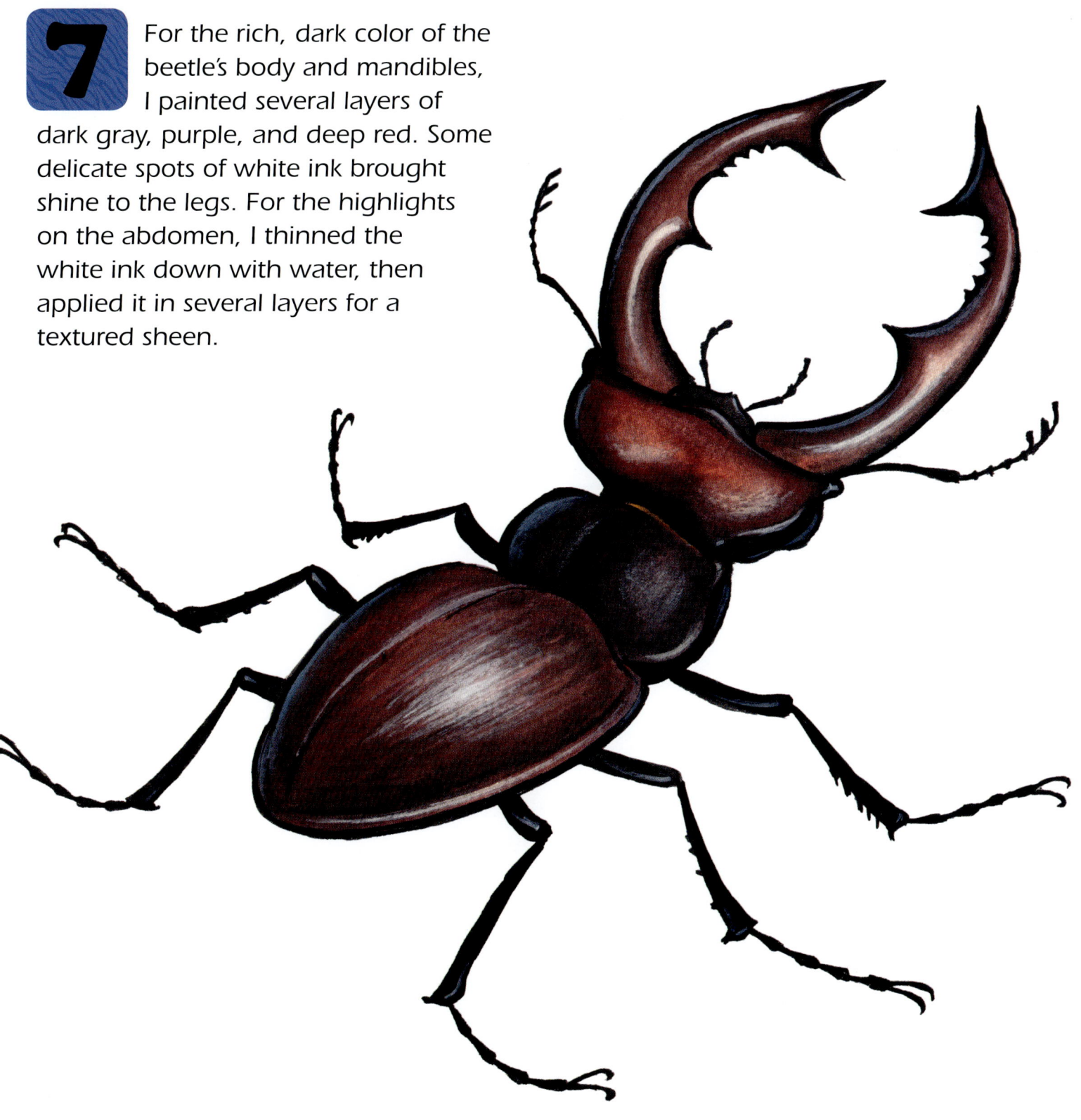

CRICKET

Crickets are related to grasshoppers. and like grasshoppers, they can hop! They have long, powerful back legs, specially adapted for jumping. In many places, crickets are believed to bring happiness and good luck, and in some parts of Asia, they are kept as pets.

1 The cricket's thorax and abdomen are connected to make one body section. So the first stage is to draw two shapes—a small oval head and much larger, pointy-ended oval for the body. Make sure you leave enough space on the page for the legs and antennae.

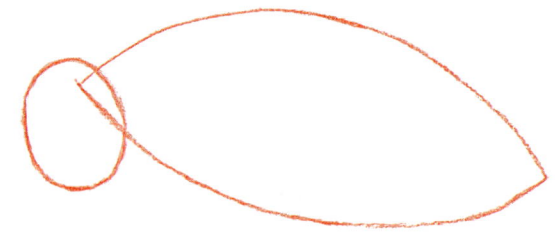

2 Start the legs by figuring out where they join the body, and then draw in the upper parts, overlapping them where necessary. Add the upper parts of the legs on the far side where they are visible above the body and head. Add the tail and the mouthparts.

CHIRPY CRICKET

At night, male crickets sing a chirping song to attract female crickets. They do this by rubbing one wing against another. The edges of the wings have teeth like a comb, which make the sound. The cricket shown in our illustration would not be able to chirp, because it has not yet grown wings

ANIMAL FACTS

3 Draw the lower parts of the legs, then work on the details of the body and head. Add the antennae as two stumps coming out of the forehead.

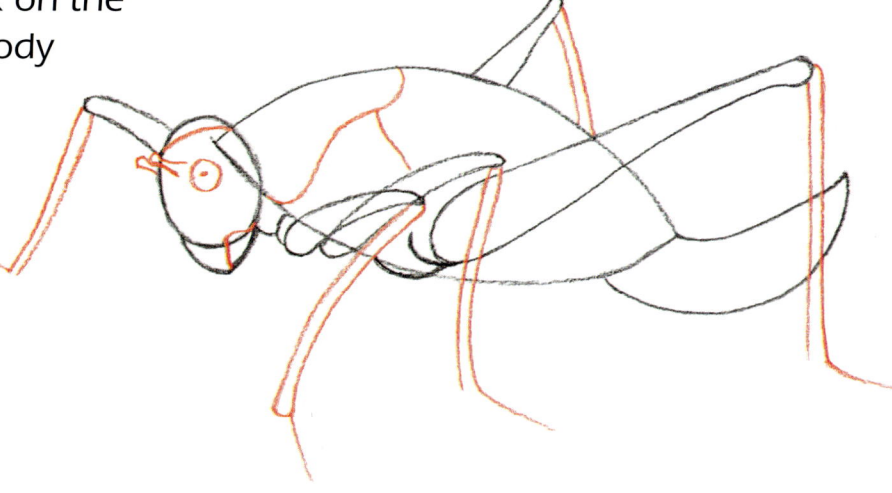

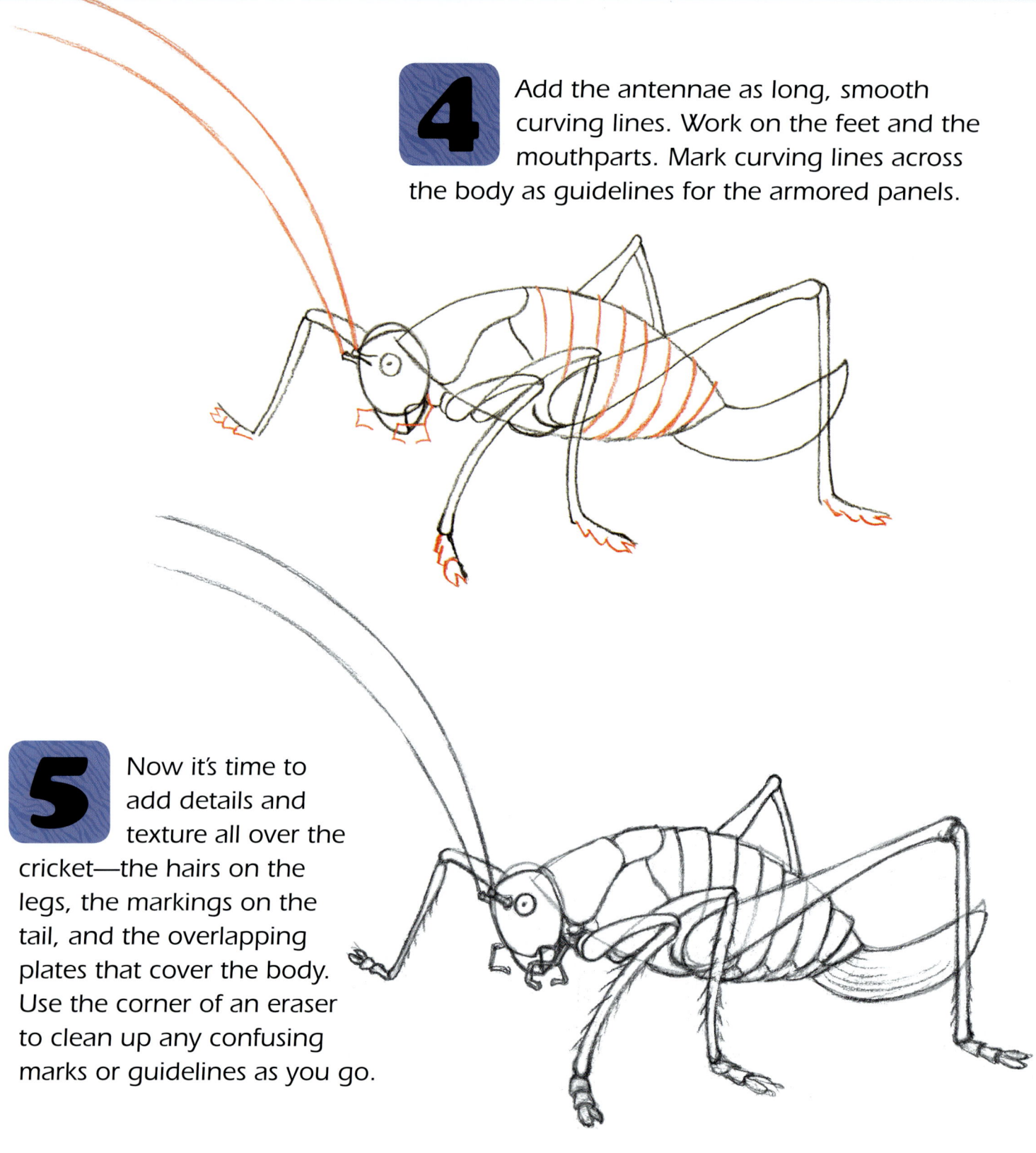

4 Add the antennae as long, smooth curving lines. Work on the feet and the mouthparts. Mark curving lines across the body as guidelines for the armored panels.

5 Now it's time to add details and texture all over the cricket—the hairs on the legs, the markings on the tail, and the overlapping plates that cover the body. Use the corner of an eraser to clean up any confusing marks or guidelines as you go.

6 To capture the rich coloring of the cricket, I used green and yellow as my outline colors, with a touch of black for the darkest parts. Be careful when inking around parts that overlap others—start with the parts closest to you and work backward.

7 For the coloring, I used dark blue mixed with *green* for the *shading*, then various bright greens for the body. I added a touch of reddish brown on the head, upper back, and lower legs, together with some yellow.

HONEYBEE

Bees live on the **nectar** and **pollen** produced by flowering plants. Honeybees are a particular type of bee that make honey from the nectar they collect and store it in a honeycomb. Only female bees make honey.

1 Start with the three main body parts: an upside-down egg shape for the head, a circle for the thorax, and a large oval for the abdomen. Make sure you leave spaces in between.

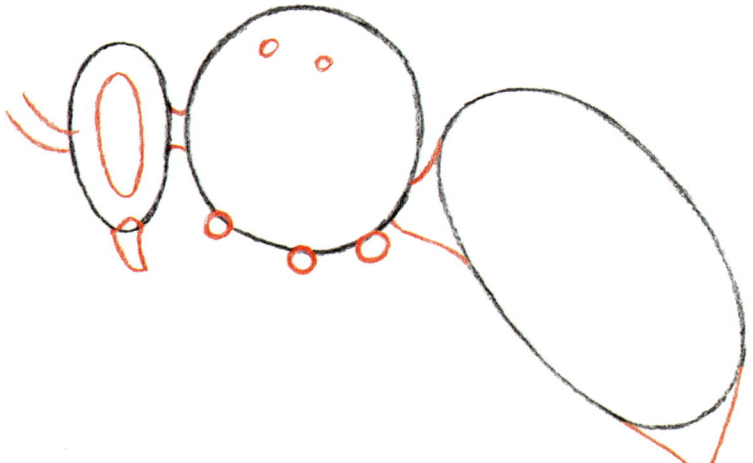

2 Connect the body parts and add the sting at the end of the abdomen. Then draw the large oval eye and the mouth shape. Mark the places where the legs and wings join the thorax with small circles.

DRONES AND WORKERS

Male bees, or drones, don't collect nectar or pollen. It's up to the female worker bees to do all the hard work—collecting nectar, cleaning up, and guarding the hive (the bees' home). Queen honeybees rule the hive and can lay up to 2,000 eggs in one day!

ANIMAL FACTS

 Our honeybee is in the flying position. Each leg points away from the body at a different angle, then slopes downward and backward after the first joint. The wings can be rough shapes, the upper one being much larger than the lower one.

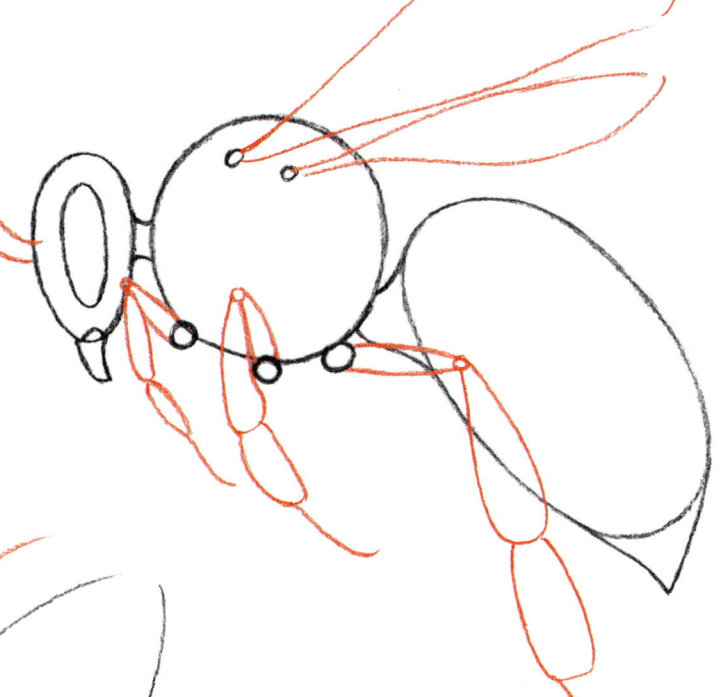

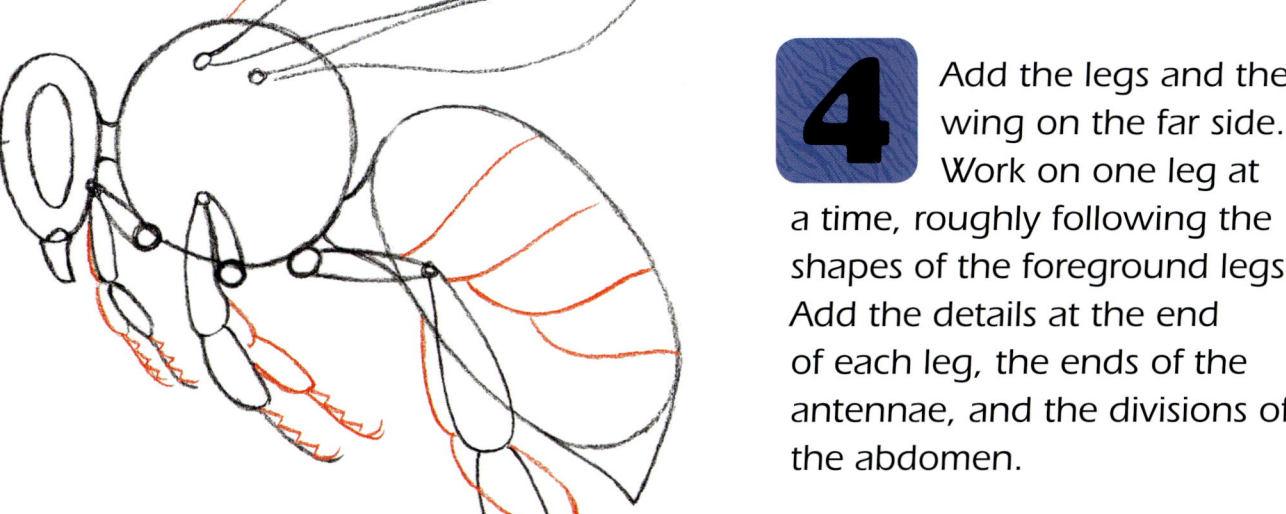

 Add the legs and the wing on the far side. Work on one leg at a time, roughly following the shapes of the foreground legs. Add the details at the end of each leg, the ends of the antennae, and the divisions of the abdomen.

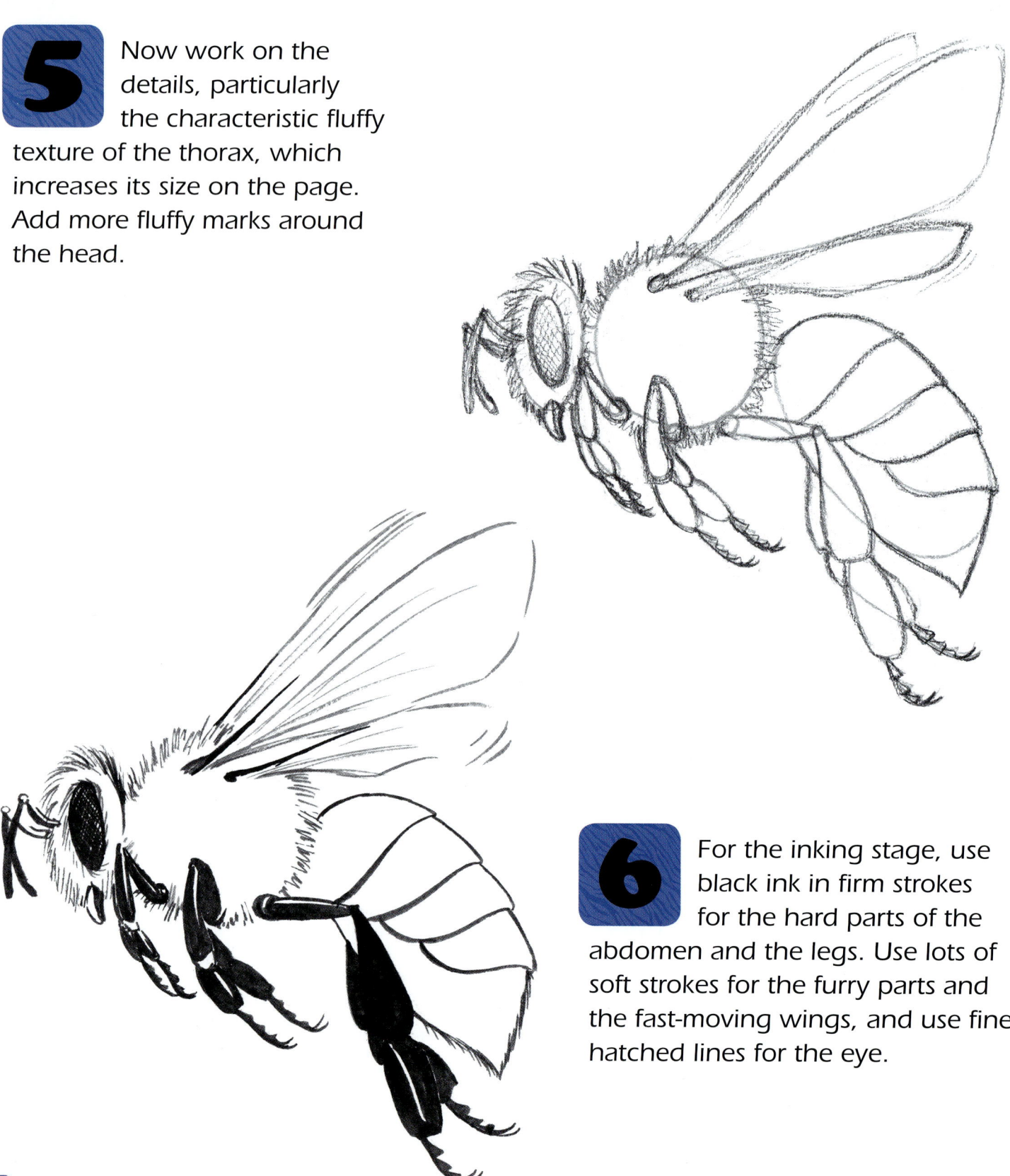

5 Now work on the details, particularly the characteristic fluffy texture of the thorax, which increases its size on the page. Add more fluffy marks around the head.

6 For the inking stage, use black ink in firm strokes for the hard parts of the abdomen and the legs. Use lots of soft strokes for the furry parts and the fast-moving wings, and use fine hatched lines for the eye.

7 To color the bee, I used layers of browns and yellows for the thorax and head, to build up a textured feel. The blurry wings needed only a few swift strokes. The abdomen took a little longer, as I blended black stripes into the yellow. For the highlights, I used tiny, soft strokes for the fluffy parts and bold, shiny marks for the smooth abdomen.

A COUNTRY SCENE

Now it's time to bring together the skills you have learned in this book and put your insects into a countryside scene. I chose a bank of wildflowers as a suitable background scene for butterflies and bees. I did lots of small, rough drawings before selecting one to work up in greater detail.

1 When you are creating a scene, it is a good idea to start with a rough version of your artwork. To allow for close-up drawings of the insects, I chose a low eye level. This means that the fence is above eye level, disappearing toward the distant horizon. A cottage provides some interest.

2 Next, I quickly washed on some watercolors to establish a rough color scheme. I also decided on a light source—bright sunshine coming from the right—and shaded the scene with that in mind.

3 Still working on my color rough, I used dark ink to strengthen parts of the drawing and white ink to make some features clearer. I decided that the top right part of the picture was a little empty, so I added more trees. I also added a patch of shade to the road, to provide a darker background behind the colorful flowers.

4 Use your color rough as a guide to map out your scene on good paper. First, I established the curves that run through the picture and the main features of the drawing. The aim of this stage is to place the elements on the page, so everything can be drawn quite loosely.

5 Much of the detail in this scene will be added in the inking and painting stages. There's no need to draw each blade of grass. However, the cottage and the insects need good guidelines if they are going to look convincing. It is also important to get the spacing right between the fence posts to give a sense of distance.

6 Next, add detail to the insects and cottage, as well as the larger flowers. The flowers need not be precisely detailed, but they should have some individual characteristics.

7 For the inking stage, I decided to use very little black ink, keeping it for just the insects to make them stand out. To keep the picture bright, I inked the foliage with green, the poppies with dark red, and the wooden details with dark brown. I used some strokes of purple watercolor for a faint horizon.

8 Using my color rough, I was able to add color and shade quickly and confidently. Once the main colors were blocked in, I mixed white ink into yellows and greens to layer some lighter grass over darker areas. I mixed white in with red for highlights on the poppies. Then I added some daisies on top of the grass.

GLOSSARY

antennae (an-TEH-nee) Two long, thin parts attached to the head of an insect, used for sensing touch or smell.

larvae (LAHR-vee) The earliest life stage of some insects, which often looks very different from the adult insects.

nectar (NEK-tur) A sweet liquid produced by flowering plants.

neutral (NOO-trul) In painting, a shade that matches well with most other colors.

symmetrical (sih-MEH-trih-kul) Describes something that is the same on both sides of a center point or line.

WEBSITES

Due to the changing nature of Internet links, PowerKids Press has developed an online list of websites related to the subject of this book. This site is updated regularly. Please use this link to access the list:

www.powerkidslinks.com/HTDA/insect

FURTHER READING

Ames, Lee J. and Ray Burns. *Draw 50 Creepy Crawlies.* New York: Watson-Guptill, 2013.

Regan, Lisa and Steve Roberts. *How to Draw Bugs.* London, England: Miles Kelly Publishing, 2008.

Tait, Noel. *Insects & Spiders.* New York: Simon & Schuster, 2008.

INDEX